The Spirit Of Rebellion

Bliss

Published by Bliss, 2025.

THE SPIRIT OF REBELLION

First edition. February 19, 2025.

Copyright © 2025 Bliss.

ISBN: 979-8230416906

Written by Bliss.

Table of Contents

God resists the proud ,He exalts the humble

God resists the proud ,He exalts the humble

PREFACE

Doubt when it is fully grown, gives way to active spiritual rebellion. Our fight is a fight of faith, steeling against unbelief and the moment we let doubt into our hearts and allow it to grow, our fight ceases and our rebellion begins.

I think for me it started in my days in High School, a general lack of contentment started to build in my life. A desire for something different, a dissatisfaction or boredom with my life. A disillusionment with how it had all turned out and the more I thought about it the more I was dissatisfied with my home, my family, my school, my career, the general direction my life was taking.

It developed a habit of doubt in me, calling into question everything I had learnt about God from His word, I stopped believing. And slowly rebellion crawled into my heart without me realizing it. Rebellion increased giving way to pride, a lack of love, a lack of faith, a lack of trust in God. I entertained the lie in my heart that God did not love me.

I even contemplated leaving Christianity to either becoming an atheist or just joking another religion.

Elevated my own goals and became so wrapped up in myself there was not room for God. I built my own principles and beliefs contrary to the word of God,I lived on human wisdom and what I believed according to my own understanding.

I thought life was well with me and that I didn't even want to listen to any preachings and teachings .

I was dying inside while trying to live to my own understanding,

God is His mercy and grace came after me ,and saved me from that rebellious life ,and He is still working on me seven years down the line.

So it's possible that you too can overcome that evil spirit through Jesus Christ.This is the best decision you have chosen ,accepting Christ to work on you .

Isaiah 30 addresses rebellion (KJV)

1 Woe to the rebellious children, saith the LORD, that take counsel, but not of me; and that cover with a covering, but not of my spirit, that they may add sin to sin:

2 That walk to go down into Egypt, and have not asked at my mouth; to strengthen themselves in the strength of Pharaoh, and to trust in the shadow of Egypt! (The rebellious run to the ungodly for advise, counseling and support)

3 Therefore shall the strength of Pharaoh be your shame, and the trust in the shadow of Egypt your confusion.

4 For his princes were at Zoan, and his ambassadors came to Hanes.

5 They were all ashamed of a people that could not profit them, nor be a help nor profit, but a shame, and also a reproach.

6 The burden of the beasts of the south: into the land of trouble and anguish, from whence come the young and old lion, the viper and fiery flying serpent, they will carry their riches upon the shoulders of young asses, and their treasures upon the bunches of camels, to a people that shall not profit them.

7 For the Egyptians shall help in vain, and to no purpose: therefore have I cried concerning this, Their strength is to sit still.

8 Now go, write it before them in a table, and note it in a book, that it may be for the time to come forever and ever:

9 That this is a rebellious people, lying children, children that will not hear the law of the LORD:

10 Which say to the seers, See not; and to the prophets, Prophesy not unto us right things, speak unto us smooth things, prophesy deceits:

11 Get you out of the way, turn aside out of the path, cause the Holy One of Israel to cease from before us.

12 Wherefore thus saith the Holy One of Israel, Because ye despise this word, and trust in oppression and perverseness, and stay thereon:

13 Therefore this iniquity shall be to you as a breach ready to fall, swelling out in a high wall, whose breaking cometh suddenly at an instant.

14 And he shall break it as the breaking of the potter's vessel that is broken in pieces; he shall not spare: so that there shall not be found in the bursting of it a shard to take fire from the hearth, or to take water withal out of the pit.

15 For thus saith the Lord GOD, the Holy One of Israel; In returning and rest shall ye be saved; in quietness and in confidence shall be your strength: and ye would not.

16 But ye said, No; for we will flee upon horses; therefore shall ye flee: and, We will ride upon the swift; therefore shall they that pursue you be swift.

17 One thousand shall flee at the rebuke of one; at the rebuke of five shall ye flee: till ye be left as a beacon upon the top of a mountain, and as an ensign on a hill.

INTRODUCTION

You must be very familiar with the word rebellion .Rebellion is a vice that limits us in relationships and in our journey towards success in life.

We have various definitions of the term rebellion .

Let's take a look at what are the different definitions of the term Rebellion

Definitions from Oxford Languages ·

noun

an act of armed resistance to an established government or leader.
"the authorities put down a rebellion by landless colonials"
Similar:

- uprising

- revolt

- insurrection

- riot

- civil disobedience

- civil disorder

- unrest

- anarchy

The action or process of resisting authority, control, or convention.
"an act of teenage rebellion"
Similar:

- defiance

- disobedience

In the Bible, rebellion is defined as **disobedience to God, or opposition to God's authority, Word, and appointed authorities.** It is considered a sin and a downfall for humanity.

What's the meaning of "The spirit of Rebellion'?

The spirit of rebellion" refers to a mindset or attitude of defiance and disobedience against authority, often associated with a strong desire to resist rules, commands, or established norms, essentially meaning someone who actively opposes and challenges those in power; in religious contexts, it is often seen as a negative force going against God's authority.

Key points about the "spirit of rebellion":

✓Opposition to authority:

The core element of a rebellious spirit is actively going against established power structures or rules.

✓Pride and defiance:

People with a rebellious spirit often exhibit a sense of pride and unwillingness to submit to others.

Religious interpretation:

In some religious beliefs, the "spirit of rebellion" is considered a negative force, representing disobedience against God.

Rebellion opens doors for Satan to come in and wreak havoc in our lives. It blinds us to the truth and keeps us in opposition to God. When we are in rebellion, we walk and live contrary to the word of God; not willing to yield to God's will or His commands.

1 Samuel 15:23 (NKJV) "For rebellion is as the sin of witchcraft, And stubbornness is as iniquity and idolatry. Because you have rejected the word of the Lord, He also has rejected you from being king."

THE SPIRIT OF REBELLION

Proverbs 7:11 (NKJV) "She was loud and rebellious, Her feet would not stay at home.

Many, if not all, rebels are psychologically driven by a false sense of superiority and wounded sense of powerlessness stemming from early childhood experiences. Their rebelliousness can be seen as a compensatory mechanism. If you understand this, it can help you feel compassion for the rebel.

To overcome the spirit of rebellion, we must remember that God must be exalted more than the rebellion. Instead of rehearsing all of the negative things that the person is doing, begin to decree God's word and his blessings over their lives.

We will delve deeper and discuss more about this spirit of rebellion in the Biblical perspective .

We are no different to Adam and Eve who wanted a bigger, better, more powerful version of themselves, of God even. They wanted more than the life they had; they declared their lives as being inadequate. They made a choice for something other than God had given them.

Perhaps your life has not turned out like you expected it to:

- Choices were made for you that you had no control over

- Circumstances have happened that you did not ask for

- Relationships or situations have fallen on you because you had no-one to consult with

- It seems that you are in dead end circumstances

When one is living a life over which you have no control, it is easy to blame the ONE who did have control i.e. God. WE start to question everything about His character. And rebellion starts to rise in us.

Spiritual rebellion rejects the life God has given you. It births a self-hate that says "I hate my life and who I am." We judge our lives as worthless and thereby judge the God of the universe as worthless.

Rebellion is an attitude that resists authority. It resists God's divinely instituted order. The first act of rebellion against God's order of things, was from the devil himself and he took one third of the angels with him.

Spiritual rebellion is to elevate your agenda above the agenda of God, and it has one purpose – to block one from thriving and pressing into God.

Understanding the underlying reasons behind rebellion is crucial to overcoming its hold on us and embracing a life of purpose.

When we choose a path of rebellion, we risk distancing ourselves from the abundant blessings God desires for us.

It's not about a harsh punishment but rather the natural outcome of turning away from the guidance and wisdom found in God's Word.

A rebellious life can create a wedge between us and the joy that comes from a close relationship with God.

Psalm 51:10 speaks of a desire for a pure heart and a steadfast spirit – qualities that are contrary to a rebellious spirit.

As Christians, our aim is to align our lives with God's will, and when we rebel, we jeopardize the intimacy and peace that flourish in a life surrendered to Him.

It's a gentle reminder to continually seek God's forgiveness, guidance, and grace, allowing His love to shape our actions and choices.

We should align our actions and decisions with our values and aspirations.

Purpose provides us with a sense of direction, meaning, and fulfillment.

It gives our lives a greater sense of significance and allows us to make a positive impact on the world around us.

Discovering our purpose requires self-reflection.

THE SPIRIT OF REBELLION

Embracing a life of purpose often begins with a journey of self-reflection, a process that invites us to explore the depths of our hearts and align our desires with God's plan for us.

Just as Psalm 139:23-24 encourages us to search our hearts and know our anxieties, self-reflection is a vital tool for understanding our motivations and aspirations.

CHAPTER ONE

' Lucifers Rebellion

According to the Bible, Lucifer, or Satan, was originally one of Gods most beautiful and powerful angels. He was created as a cherub, a type of angelic being associated with divine knowledge and wisdom. However, Lucifers pride and desire for power led him to rebel against God.

Ezekiel 28:11-19(NKJV)

Ezekiel 28:11

Moreover the word of the Lord came to me, saying,

Ezekiel 28:12 "Son of man, take up a lamentation for the king of Tyre, and say to him, 'Thus says the Lord God:

"You were the seal of perfection,

Full of wisdom and perfect in beauty.

Ezekiel 28:13 You were in Eden, the garden of God;

Every precious stone was your covering:

The sardius, topaz, and diamond,

Beryl, onyx, and jasper,

Sapphire, turquoise, and emerald with gold.

The workmanship of your timbrels and pipes

Was prepared for you on the day you were created.

Ezekiel 28:14 "You were the anointed cherub who covers;

I established you;

You were on the holy mountain of God;

You walked back and forth in the midst of fiery stones.

Ezekiel 28:15 You were perfect in your ways from the day you were created,

Till iniquity was found in you.

Ezekiel 28:16 "By the abundance of your trading

You became filled with violence within,

And you sinned;

Therefore I cast you as a profane thing

Out of the mountain of God;
And I destroyed you, O covering cherub,
From the midst of the fiery stones.
Ezekiel 28:17 "Your heart was lifted up because of your beauty;
You corrupted your wisdom for the sake of your splendor;
I cast you to the ground,
I laid you before kings,
That they might gaze at you.
Ezekiel 28:18 "You defiled your sanctuaries
By the multitude of your iniquities,
By the iniquity of your trading;
Therefore I brought fire from your midst;
It devoured you,
And I turned you to ashes upon the earth
In the sight of all who saw you.
Ezekiel 28:19 All who knew you among the peoples are astonished at you;
You have become a horror,
And shall be no more forever.""""

Lucifer apparently became so impressed with his own beauty, intelligence, power, and position that he began to desire for himself the honor and glory that belonged to God alone. The sin that corrupted Lucifer was self-generated pride.This was a clear act of rebellion to his creator,God.

In another text from the Bible ,in the book of Isaiah 14

Isaiah 14:12 (NKJV)

"How you are fallen from heaven,

O Lucifer, son of the morning!

How you are cut down to the ground,

You who weakened the nations!

Isaiah 14:13 For you have said in your heart:

'I will ascend into heaven,

I will exalt my throne above the stars of God;

I will also sit on the mount of the congregation

On the farthest sides of the north;

Isaiah 14:14 I will ascend above the heights of the clouds,

I will be like the Most High.'

Isaiah 14:15 Yet you shall be brought down to Sheol,

To the lowest depths of the Pit.

Isaiah 14:16 "Those who see you will gaze at you,

And consider you, saying:

'Is this the man who made the earth tremble,

Who shook kingdoms,

Isaiah 14:17 Who made the world as a wilderness

And destroyed its cities,

Who did not open the house of his prisoners?'

The five "I wills" in Isaiah 14 indicate an element of pride.

As a result of this heinous sin against God, Lucifer was banished from living in heaven (Isaiah 14:12). He became corrupt, and his name changed from Lucifer ("morning star") to Satan ("adversary"). His power became completely perverted (Isaiah 14:12,16,17). And his destiny, following the second coming of Christ, is to be bound in a pit during the 1000-year millennial kingdom over which Christ will rule

(:**Revelation 20:3 and he cast him into the bottomless pit, and shut him up, and set a seal on him, so that he should deceive the nations no more till the thousand years were finished. But after these things he must be released for a little while.**),

and eventually will be thrown into the lake of fire

(**Matthew 25:41 "Then He will also say to those on the left hand, 'Depart from Me, you cursed, into the everlasting fire prepared for the devil and his angels:**).

Consequences of Lucifers Rebellion

The consequences of Lucifer's rebellion, according to the Bible texts, include his expulsion from heaven, becoming known as Satan, the introduction of evil and sin into the world, the corruption of creation, and the ability to tempt and deceive humans, essentially marking the beginning of spiritual conflict between good and evil.

Key points about the consequences:

- Loss of Heavenly Status:

Lucifer, once a high-ranking angel, was cast out of heaven due to his pride and desire to be equal to God.

- Transformation into Satan:

After his fall, Lucifer became known as Satan, the adversary of God, with the primary goal of opposing God's will.

- Creation of Evil:

Lucifer's rebellion is seen as the origin of evil in the world, bringing corruption and sin into existence.

- Temptation of Humans:

Satan is often depicted as the tempter who seeks to lead humans astray from God's path.

- Fallen Angels:

Other angels who followed Lucifer in his rebellion are also considered "fallen angels" and are often associated with demonic forces.

Identifying someone with the "spirit of Lucifer" is often based on observing behavioral patterns that exhibit characteristics like

- excessive pride,
- self-centeredness,
- a desire for power and control,
- manipulation of others,
- open rebellion against authority, and
- a disregard for morality, often accompanied by a strong attraction to dark or occult practices;

However, it's important to note that directly discerning someone's spiritual state is considered highly subjective and should be approached with caution and sensitivity.

Key signs often associated with a "Luciferian spirit":

1. Extreme pride and arrogance: A constant need for admiration and a sense of superiority over others.
2. Desire for power and control: Seeking to dominate situations and people around them.
3. Deception and manipulation: Using cunning tactics to achieve personal goals, often at the expense of others.
4. Rebellious attitude: Open defiance against rules, authority figures, and societal norms.

On an individual basis it's always an important decision to examine your character and do an honest view of your behaviour ,ask the holy spirit to reveal to you and expose such traits

The spirit of Rebellion without careful examination ,may destroy you and your destiny.

Instead of "please speak to me", pray "Lord help me receive & obey your word." "Forgive me of being in rebellion against your word." "I may not even understand your command but I surrender my life to your command."

I want you to know however, that rebellion is more than a decision, rebellion is a spirit.

Biblical Approach to Dealing with this kind of rebellious spirit

Even if everyone else is doing it. Rebellious people often try to justify themselves by gathering seemingly credible people to be in agreement with their opposition to authority. ...

- Embrace your authority. According to the Word of God ,Authority is from God,opposing Authority is opposing God ,and that is rebellion.

Let's all purpose to honor Authority as it pleases God when we do so .We may not like the one in authority ,but that shouldn't be a reason to rebel against him or her,as a child of God ,play your part and let God do the rest .

- Lean on God's truth. Gods truth is in the word ,The Holy Book.You shall know the truth and the truth shall set you free Incase you have questions concerning a particular thing you do not understand,always turn to the word of God ,you will find solution and how to deal with it.

- Equip yourself with prayer.Prayer is a weapon ,prayer is a sign of humility ,when you pray God listens and comes to our aid.Whatever it is you are battling with,it could be pride,self centeredness etc ,seek God in prayer and He will help you deal with that wicked spirit.

CHAPTER TWO

KING SAULS REBELLION

1 Samuel 15:1-30

Samuel also said to Saul, "The Lord sent me to anoint you king over His people, over Israel. Now therefore, heed the voice of the words of the Lord.

1 Samuel 15:2 Thus says the Lord of hosts: 'I will punish Amalek for what he did to Israel, how he ambushed him on the way when he came up from Egypt.

1 Samuel 15:3 Now go and attack Amalek, and utterly destroy all that they have, and do not spare them. But kill both man and woman, infant and nursing child, ox and sheep, camel and donkey.'"

1 Samuel 15:4 So Saul gathered the people together and numbered them in Telaim, two hundred thousand foot soldiers and ten thousand men of Judah.

1 Samuel 15:5 And Saul came to a city of Amalek, and lay in wait in the valley.

1 Samuel 15:6 Then Saul said to the Kenites, "Go, depart, get down from among the Amalekites, lest I destroy you with them. For you showed kindness to all the children of Israel when they came up out of Egypt." So the Kenites departed from among the Amalekites.

1 Samuel 15:7 And Saul attacked the Amalekites, from Havilah all the way to Shur, which is east of Egypt.

1 Samuel 15:8 He also took Agag king of the Amalekites alive, and utterly destroyed all the people with the edge of the sword.

1 Samuel 15:9 But Saul and the people spared Agag and the best of the sheep, the oxen, the fatlings, the lambs, and all that was good, and were unwilling to utterly destroy them. But everything despised and worthless, that they utterly destroyed.

1 Samuel 15:10 Saul Rejected as King

Now the word of the Lord came to Samuel, saying,

1 Samuel 15:11 "I greatly regret that I have set up Saul as king, for he has turned back from following Me, and has not performed My commandments." And it grieved Samuel, and he cried out to the Lord all night.

1 Samuel 15:12 So when Samuel rose early in the morning to meet Saul, it was told Samuel, saying, "Saul went to Carmel, and indeed, he set up a monument for himself; and he has gone on around, passed by, and gone down to Gilgal."

1 Samuel 15:13 Then Samuel went to Saul, and Saul said to him, "Blessed are you of the Lord! I have performed the commandment of the Lord."

1 Samuel 15:14 But Samuel said, "What then is this bleating of the sheep in my ears, and the lowing of the oxen which I hear?"

1 Samuel 15:15 And Saul said, "They have brought them from the Amalekites; for the people spared the best of the sheep and the oxen, to sacrifice to the Lord your God; and the rest we have utterly destroyed."

1 Samuel 15:16 Then Samuel said to Saul, "Be quiet! And I will tell you what the Lord said to me last night."

And he said to him, "Speak on."

1 Samuel 15:17 So Samuel said, "When you were little in your own eyes, were you not head of the tribes of Israel? And did not the Lord anoint you king over Israel?

1 Samuel 15:18 Now the Lord sent you on a mission, and said, 'Go, and utterly destroy the sinners, the Amalekites, and fight against them until they are consumed.'

1 Samuel 15:19 Why then did you not obey the voice of the Lord? Why did you swoop down on the spoil, and do evil in the sight of the Lord?"

1 Samuel 15:20 And Saul said to Samuel, "But I have obeyed the voice of the Lord, and gone on the mission on which the Lord sent

me, and brought back Agag king of Amalek; I have utterly destroyed the Amalekites.

1 Samuel 15:21 But the people took of the plunder, sheep and oxen, the best of the things which should have been utterly destroyed, to sacrifice to the Lord your God in Gilgal."

1 Samuel 15:22 So Samuel said:

"Has the Lord as great delight in burnt offerings and sacrifices,

As in obeying the voice of the Lord?

Behold, to obey is better than sacrifice,

And to heed than the fat of rams.

1 Samuel 15:23 For rebellion is as the sin of witchcraft,

And stubbornness is as iniquity and idolatry.

Because you have rejected the word of the Lord,

He also has rejected you from being king."

1 Samuel 15:24 Then Saul said to Samuel, "I have sinned, for I have transgressed the commandment of the Lord and your words, because I feared the people and obeyed their voice.

1 Samuel 15:25 Now therefore, please pardon my sin, and return with me, that I may worship the Lord."

1 Samuel 15:26 But Samuel said to Saul, "I will not return with you, for you have rejected the word of the Lord, and the Lord has rejected you from being king over Israel."

1 Samuel 15:27 And as Samuel turned around to go away, Saul seized the edge of his robe, and it tore.

1 Samuel 15:28 So Samuel said to him, "The Lord has torn the kingdom of Israel from you today, and has given it to a neighbor of yours, who is better than you.

1 Samuel 15:29 And also the Strength of Israel will not lie nor relent. For He is not a man, that He should relent."

1 Samuel 15:30 Then he said, "I have sinned; yet honor me now, please, before the elders of my people and before Israel, and return with me, that I may worship the Lord your God."

If you had asked Saul, "Do you see yourself rebelling against God after you become a king?", I'm sure he would have given you a resounding, "No, absolutely not!".

The reality is that most Christians don't choose to just one day walk in rebellion against God, but they find themselves one step at a time compromising God's commandments which leads them to disobedience.

1Samuel 15:3,9

God didn't give Saul a reason as to why he should destroy everything, but He did give him specific instructions to destroy everything that the Amalekites owned including their king Agag.

Saul used his own judgment as to what should be saved and what should be destroyed. Naturally, it only made sense to get rid of worthless things but save valuable spoils.

Many times the things of the spirit will not make sense in the natural. This is when we have to make a decision to walk in the spirit and not lean on our own understanding.

1Samuel 15:12

After his great victory, Saul became delusional. He told Samuel that he had actually performed the commandment of the Lord. The truth was that he performed only part of the commandment but not all of it. Partial obedience is still disobedience!

Full obedience is a challenge to all of us. The Lord asks us to do something, but we do it partially to the degree that makes sense or is beneficial to us. The portion that we don't like or it doesn't benefit us, we try to ignore it or justify it.

Saul deceived himself by believing that he was obedient to God, and as a result he confidently lied to Samuel about having followed God's commandment.

To avoid self-deception, we need to love the truth more than ourselves. Otherwise we will give leeway to ourselves when obeying God is hard or inconvenient!

THE SPIRIT OF REBELLION

As a direct result of this disobedience we see Saul lose the kingdom and also the fellowship of Samuel.

What can we learn from this text

1) Rebellion is as the sin of witchcraft (verse 23)

Note that a stubborn and rebellious child under the law were under the penalty of death (Deuteronomy 21:18-20 **If a man has a stubborn and rebellious son who will not obey the voice of his father or the voice of his mother, and who, when they have chastened him, will not heed them,19 then his father and his mother shall take hold of him and bring him out to the elders of his city, to the gate of his city.20 And they shall say to the elders of his city, 'This son of ours is stubborn and rebellious; he will not obey our voice; he is a glutton and a drunkard.'**

; Exodus 22:18 **"You shall not permit a sorceress to live.**)

Now most of us would say that we would never commit witchcraft or idolatry, but all of us rebel sometimes, whether it be against God, our parents, our bosses, or the other authorities God has placed in our lives.

2) That partial obedience is also rebellion (verse 7-9)

Note that Saul left the good animals alive and wanted to sacrifice them unto the Lord, Samuel told him that God is more pleased with obedience than sacrifice.

Many times we don't totally disobey but we do it partially, like finding ways to get around the rules or bending them in our favor etc.

Remember that idolatry is covetousness (**Colossians 3:5 Therefore put to death your members which are on the earth: fornication, uncleanness, passion, evil desire, and covetousness, which is idolatry.**), this would apply here to putting our own wants and wishes ahead of God's.

3) Even the smallest rebellion has consequences (verses 28-35)

Saul lost the kingdom and eventually his life but note also that he lost the fellowship of Samuel (verse 35).

We must weigh all the cost, remembering some bridges once burnt are very hard to rebuild.

SUMMARY

Saul let his position as king fill him up with an inflated sense of self-importance. Eventually, he even assumed that he was qualified to take on duties meant for the priests. The Lord saw each overstep, and rebuked him through Samuel.(**James 4:6 But He gives more grace. Therefore He says:**

"God resists the proud,

But gives grace to the humble.")

Saul was blessed with gifts such as confidence and passion. But pride, insecurity and impatience in certain moments led him to disregard what he knew was right, and to then try and defend himself. Because his heart was not fully given to God, he lost his position and favor.

The story of King Saul is really a cautionary tale that applies to every believer, since we all have influence on those around us. His kingship reminds us that the best earthly leaders aren't meant to take the place of God, but to point people to the true Lord of their lives.

How to overcome this type of rebellion:

- Seek God's guidance: Actively seek out God's will and guidance through prayer and studying scripture.

- Humility: Acknowledge your own limitations and be open to correction when necessary.

- Complete obedience: Follow God's commands fully, without trying to pick and choose which parts to obey.

- Repentance: If you do disobey, be quick to confess your sin and seek forgiveness.

- Trust in God's authority: Recognize that God's authority is supreme and should be respected above all else.

CHAPTER THREE

KING NEBUCHADNEZZARS REBELLION

Daniel 4:28-33(ESV)

28 All this came upon King Nebuchadnezzar.

29 At the end of twelve months he was walking on the roof of the royal palace of Babylon,

30 and the king answered and said, "Is not this great Babylon, which I have built by my mighty power as a royal residence and for the glory of my majesty?"

31 While the words were still in the king's mouth, there fell a voice from heaven, "O King Nebuchadnezzar, to you it is spoken: The kingdom has departed from you,

32 and you shall be driven from among men, and your dwelling shall be with the beasts of the field. And you shall be made to eat grass like an ox, and seven periods of time shall pass over you, until you know that the Most High rules the kingdom of men and gives it to whom he will."

33 Immediately the word was fulfilled against Nebuchadnezzar.

If you read the story about Nebuchadnezzar, in its full context, you learn God had warned him a full year in advance from this occurring. This is the goodness and mercy of God.

The fruit of pride is always seen in rebellion. God considers all disobedience an act of rebellion. Rebellion is as the sin of witchcraft and stubbornness is as the sin of idolatry. Pride exalts one's will above Gods known expressed will. We are shown the rebellion of Lucifer ~ I will ascend to heaven; above the stars of God. I will set my throne on high; I will sit on the mount of assembly in the far reaches of the North; I will ascend above the heights of the clouds; I will make myself like the Most High.

None of these places where given to Him by the Father. Iniquity was found in him. Pride of heart led the rebellion. Jesus said I saw Satan fall like lightening from heaven. God threw him out of heaven and Lucifier became Satan. In the garden he worked to deceive Adam and Eve and they rebelled. The fruit of their rebellion cost man a cursed ground to toil and separation from Gods life and the garden He had created for them to flourish in.

Our scriptures regarding Nebuchadnzeer's fall paints a story of true humiliation. In his rejection of the word God gave him, and his refusal to repent, He declares His own power and His own majesty, setting himself up for one of the mightier falls recorded in scripture .

The lesson we all can learn is to beware of anything that would tempt us not to acknowledge every good and perfect gift coming to us from the Father in His goodness and mercy.

At the end of the days I, Nebuchadnezzar, lifted my eyes to heaven, and my reason returned to me, and I blessed the Most High, and praised and honored him who lives forever, for his dominion is an everlasting dominion, and his kingdom endures from generation to generation; all the inhabitants of the earth are accounted as nothing, and he does according to his will among the host of heaven and among the inhabitants of the earth; and none can stay his hand or say to him, "What have you done?"

Selah.

Pride is an abomination to the Lord and from James and 1 Peter we find the word opposes to mean an active resistance. It was a military word used to describe the battle array of an army that came to fight. God opposes the proud but gives grace to the humble. Our admonition from James and Peter is to Humble ourselves under the mighty hand of God, with the promise, He will exalt you.

Humility hears and obeys. God instructs and we humble ourselves. Humility always agrees with God and submits to the instruction. Submission is always willing. Humility is always prepared to understand whatever God says is for our well being. God opposes the proud but gives grace to the humble. Grace must be received by faith and we can't even do that without first agreeing with God.

Philippians instructs us to have this mindset, which is ours in Christ Jesus, in other words, in Christ Jesus we won't have another mindset). Jesus made himself of no reputation, became a servant and humbled himself by becoming obedient. We can't be humble if there is no obedience. Humility is seen in the act of obedience. Pride is seen in rebellion.

CHAPTER FOUR

KING BELSHAZZARS REBELLION

In the Bible, King Belshazzar rebelled against God through pride, blasphemy, and idolatry. This rebellion led to the end of his kingdom.

The Babylonian king throws a banquet for his nobles. This was a common occurrence of the day. These parties were large and extravagant, designed to illustrate the opulence of the King. Belshazzar, however, takes things too far. As the party goes on, the King orders that the holy goblets, taken from the temple in Jerusalem, be brought to the party "so that his wives and concubines might drink from them" (Daniel 5:4). This is the height of Belshazzar's arrogance. Belshazzar takes what belongs to God and uses it for his own pleasure.

This may not seem like much, but the goblets of gold and silver had been previously consecrated to the Lord. This means they were to be used exclusively for ritual worship. They were objects set apart to bring glory and praise to Yahweh. To take God's holy vessels as a means for human drunkenness displays a complete and utter disrespect for that which belongs to God. Belshazzar assumes that he is of such an exalted status that he may use, or misuse, God's good creation for his own personal enjoyment or pleasure. Belshazzar sees himself as the rightful owner of holy things.

Daniel charges Belshazzar with "not humbling yourself but setting yourself up against the Lord of heaven" (Daniel 5:23). This is what pride creates in our spiritual lives. While we may not use sanctified objects as vehicles for human drunkenness, we can similarly misuse God's good possessions for our own purpose or glory. Whenever we act disdainfully toward that which God calls holy, we set ourselves up against the Lord of heaven and earth. We assert that our pleasure overrides God's sovereignty in life. To do so is to deny God as the rightful King over heaven and earth.

As if drinking from the holy vessels were not enough, Scripture relates that Belshazzar and his companions "praise the gods of gold and silver, of bronze, iron, wood and stone" (Daniel 5:4). In doing so, Belshazzar "did not honor the God who holds in his hand [his] life and ways" (Daniel 5:24). Belshazzar denies the power of Yahweh in his life. He believes that it is his material possessions that give him life and protect his future.

This act of praising material possessions is a direct violation of the first commandment. The commandment to "have no other gods but me" (Exodus 20:1), stands as the foundation of our life with God. This commandment is rooted in God's identity as "the Lord your God, who brought you out of Egypt, out of the land of slavery." Attributing salvation to any other being, particularly those "who cannot see or hear, or understand" (Daniel 5:23) is an insult to God's lordship in our lives.

Pride leads us to exalt ourselves. Our focus turns inward as we view ourselves in the place of God. This has always been a temptation for humanity, and stands behind the first great sin. The serpent in Genesis tempts Adam and Eve under the promise that eating the forbidden fruit will make them "like God, knowing good from evil" (Genesis 3:5). When we live from prideful arrogance, we exalt ourselves above God. We are tempted to see our own plots and strategies as that which secures our earthly and heavenly futures. Instead of salvation being received as a gift from God, given in grace and mercy, we see salvation as that which we earn or achieve by our own effort. Such an attitude completely disregards the activity of God, and the sacrifice of Jesus on the cross.

Belshazzar's pride convinced him that he would never suffer the consequences of rejecting the power of God in his life, even though this had been witnessed in the past. Belshazzar was keenly aware of the plight of Nebuchadnezzar.

Although Belshazzar knows the history of his ancestor, he believes that such humbling will never happen to him. In pride he believes himself immune from the Lord's rejection. This, of course, is not the case. In in response to his arrogant pride, Daniel declares that "God has numbered the days of your reign and brought it to an end" (Daniel 5:26). That very night, the kingdom is taken aways from Belshazzar and placed in the hands of another.

The book of Proverbs declares the well-known truth that "pride goes before destruction, a haughty spirit before the fall" (Proverbs 16:18). Pride leads us to abandon the ways of God and thereby step away from the source of eternal life. When we assert that the life before us is under our own mastery, we walk in the way of destruction. We cannot help but fall.

The story of Belshazzar depicts the damage that pride can do in our lives. We can look at Belshazzar's folly, therefore, as a way to assess our faithful witness of the Lord. For example, are we tempted to deny or misuse that which God loves? Do we see others as mere pawns for our own enjoyment? Does our devotion to God become coloured by our desire for prestige or greatness? These questions are challenging but important as they potentially expose deep or hidden sins and temptations within us.

As followers of Jesus, the servant-King, we are called to reject a spirit of pride. Our attitude should be that of Christ, "who being in the very nature of God did not consider equality with God as something to be grasped, but humbled himself" (Philippians 2:6-7). The way of self-aggrandizing arrogance is completely antithetical to the way of Jesus. Jesus did not come to be served, or to tout his own might and prowess, but to give his life as an offering to the world. This is the way of Christ and the very path we are called to walk.

CHAPTER FIVE

KING AHAB AND JEZEBELS REBELLION

King Ahab and Jezebel's "rebellion" primarily involved abandoning the worship of the God Yahweh and actively promoting the worship of Baal, a Canaanite god, through Jezebel's strong influence, leading to widespread idolatry and persecution of Yahweh's prophets within the Israelite kingdom; their actions were considered a significant deviation from God's laws and resulted in severe consequences, including a devastating drought and eventual divine judgment.

God hates rejection just as He hates rebellion. King Ahab allowed Jezebel to usurp his authority as a husband and leader and Jezebel often used his name and authority to achieve what she wanted. She manipulates and controls leadership and attempts to fill the Ahab vacuum with power plays, lies and even religious works.

Scripture Texts

1Kings 16-21

Key points about Ahab and Jezebel's rebellion:

- **Idolatry:**

Jezebel, a Phoenician princess, brought the worship of Baal to Israel, heavily influencing Ahab to establish Baal worship as a dominant religion, setting up altars and appointing Baal priests.

Their union represents a political alliance, bringing advantages to both nations. It is also an opportunity for Jezebel to foster the spread of her Baal religion with its many gods, ritual sex, and temple prostitutes. She hates the monotheistic Hebrew religion, and when she becomes queen, Israelites have already begun worshiping alien idols. Under his wife's malevolent influence, King Ahab protects and encourages pagan rituals, prompting Yahweh to inflict a three-year drought in a land where people are spurning him. Seizing the initiative, Jezebel imports 450 priests of Baal from her native Phoenicia and has many of Yahweh's prophets murdered.

To Jews, Baal worship was the worst sin against God, akin to today's Christians' embracing Satan

- **Persecution of Prophets:**

Under Jezebel's influence, many prophets of Yahweh were hunted down and killed.

Jezebel orchestrated the deaths of Yahweh's prophets and installed her own prophets of Baal to lead the people astray.

In 1 Kings 18:4, we read, "While Jezebel was killing off the Lord's prophets, Obadiah had taken a hundred prophets and hidden them in two caves, fifty in each, and had supplied them with food and water." Jezebel's actions reflected a deep-seated animosity toward God and His people.

- **Naboth's Vineyard:**

THE SPIRIT OF REBELLION

Jezebel's husband ,King Ahab covets a vineyard owned by Naboth that he wants for a garden. Naboth's refusal to sell his family inheritance sends Ahab into a funk. Jezebel asserts her dominance. "Now is the time to show yourself king over Israel," she says scornfully. "I will get the vineyard of Naboth the Jezreelite for you."

How she succeeds reinforces the eternal image of Jezebel as a scheming, murderous vixen. Forging the king's signature, she sends letters to townspeople falsely accusing Naboth of blaspheming God. When Naboth is publicly confronted, Jezebel urges the crowd: "Then take him out, and stone him to death." Naboth dies, and his property reverts to the royal family.

Jezebel's nefarious plot succeeds, but the inexorable denouement swiftly follows. Yahweh summons his prophet Elijah and instructs him to tell King Ahab that he will be punished. "Say to him: 'Would you murder and take possession? In the very place where the dogs lapped up Naboth's blood, the dogs will lap up your blood, too.' " Elijah dutifully relates Yahweh's prophecy to the king but predicts that Jezebel—not her husband—will be torn apart and eaten by dogs

- **Elijah's Confrontation:**

The prophet Elijah directly challenged Ahab and Jezebel's Baal worship, leading to dramatic confrontations.

One of the most dramatic moments of Jezebel's story is her confrontation with the prophet Elijah. After Elijah's victory over the prophets of Baal on Mount Carmel (1 Kings 18), Jezebel vowed to take Elijah's life, forcing him to flee into the wilderness. Her refusal to acknowledge the power of the one true God demonstrated her hardened heart and unrepentant nature.

- **Divine Judgement:**

Due to their blatant disregard for God's laws, Ahab and Jezebel faced severe consequences, including the prediction of their lineage being destroyed.

Jezebel's fate was foretold by the prophet Elijah. In 1 Kings 21:23, it was prophesied, "Dogs will devour Jezebel by the wall of Jezreel." This prophecy was fulfilled in 2 Kings 9 when Jezebel was thrown from a window by her own servants at the command of Jehu. Her death was a stark reminder of God's ultimate justice.

THE SPIRIT OF REBELLION

The story of King Ahab and Jezebel primarily teaches the dangers of unchecked power, the destructive influence of greed and ambition, the importance of listening to prophetic warnings, and the consequences of prioritizing personal desires over God's commands, highlighting how even powerful leaders can fall when they abandon their moral compass and succumb to evil influences like idolatry and manipulation.

This rebellious spirit of Ahab and Jezebel are destructive forces that can cause havoc in our lives and communities. However, through recognition, repentance, and deliverance, we can overcome these spirits and walk in freedom and obedience to God's Word. Remember, the power of prayer and declaration can set us free from the bondage of these spirits.

CHAPTER SIX

REBELLION OF SODOM AND GOMORRAH

In the Bible, the rebellion of Sodom and Gomorrah was a series of events that led to the destruction of the two cities by God. The cities were known for their wickedness, including sexual abuse, rape, and indecent assault.

Genesis 19:1 Sodom's Depravity

Now the two angels came to Sodom in the evening, and Lot was sitting in the gate of Sodom. When Lot saw them, he rose to meet them, and he bowed himself with his face toward the ground.

Genesis 19:2 And he said, "Here now, my lords, please turn in to your servant's house and spend the night, and wash your feet; then you may rise early and go on your way."

And they said, "No, but we will spend the night in the open square."

Genesis 19:3 But he insisted strongly; so they turned in to him and entered his house. Then he made them a feast, and baked unleavened bread, and they ate.

Genesis 19:4 Now before they lay down, the men of the city, the men of Sodom, both old and young, all the people from every quarter, surrounded the house.

Genesis 19:5 And they called to Lot and said to him, "Where are the men who came to you tonight? Bring them out to us that we may know them carnally."

Genesis 19:6 So Lot went out to them through the doorway, shut the door behind him,

Genesis 19:7 and said, "Please, my brethren, do not do so wickedly!

Genesis 19:8 See now, I have two daughters who have not known a man; please, let me bring them out to you, and you may do to them as you wish; only do nothing to these men, since this is the reason they have come under the shadow of my roof."

Genesis 19:9 And they said, "Stand back!" Then they said, "This one came in to stay here, and he keeps acting as a judge; now we will deal worse with you than with them." So they pressed hard against the man Lot, and came near to break down the door.

Genesis 19:10 But the men reached out their hands and pulled Lot into the house with them, and shut the door.

Genesis 19:11 And they struck the men who were at the doorway of the house with blindness, both small and great, so that they became weary trying to find the door.

Genesis 19:12 Sodom and Gomorrah Destroyed

Then the men said to Lot, "Have you anyone else here? Son-in-law, your sons, your daughters, and whomever you have in the city—take them out of this place!

Genesis 19:13 For we will destroy this place, because the outcry against them has grown great before the face of the Lord, and the Lord has sent us to destroy it."

Genesis 19:14 So Lot went out and spoke to his sons-in-law, who had married his daughters, and said, "Get up, get out of this place; for the Lord will destroy this city!" But to his sons-in-law he seemed to be joking.

Genesis 19:15 When the morning dawned, the angels urged Lot to hurry, saying, "Arise, take your wife and your two daughters who are here, lest you be consumed in the punishment of the city."

Genesis 19:16 And while he lingered, the men took hold of his hand, his wife's hand, and the hands of his two daughters, the Lord being merciful to him, and they brought him out and set him outside the city.

Genesis 19:17 So it came to pass, when they had brought them outside, that he said, "Escape for your life! Do not look behind you nor stay anywhere in the plain. Escape to the mountains, lest you be destroyed."

Genesis 19:18 Then Lot said to them, "Please, no, my lords!

Genesis 19:19 Indeed now, your servant has found favor in your sight, and you have increased your mercy which you have shown me by saving my life; but I cannot escape to the mountains, lest some evil overtake me and I die.

Genesis 19:20 See now, this city is near enough to flee to, and it is a little one; please let me escape there (is it not a little one?) and my soul shall live."

Genesis 19:21 And he said to him, "See, I have favored you concerning this thing also, in that I will not overthrow this city for which you have spoken.

Genesis 19:22 Hurry, escape there. For I cannot do anything until you arrive there."

Therefore the name of the city was called Zoar.

Genesis 19:23 The sun had risen upon the earth when Lot entered Zoar.

Genesis 19:24 Then the Lord rained brimstone and fire on Sodom and Gomorrah, from the Lord out of the heavens.

Genesis 19:25 So He overthrew those cities, all the plain, all the inhabitants of the cities, and what grew on the ground.

Genesis 19:28 Then he looked toward Sodom and Gomorrah, and toward all the land of the plain; and he saw, and behold, the smoke of the land which went up like the smoke of a furnace.

Genesis 19:29 And it came to pass, when God destroyed the cities of the plain, that God remembered Abraham, and sent Lot out of the midst of the overthrow, when He overthrew the cities in which Lot had dwelt.

Through the story of these cities, we see that the mercy shown to Lot was directly linked to Abraham's prayers and petitions. Abraham's prayers mattered. So when God destroyed the cities of the plain, he remembered Abraham, and he brought Lot out of the catastrophe that overthrew the cities where Lot had lived (Genesis 19:29). Oh, the power of the praying saint

(James 5:16 Confess your trespasses to one another, and pray for one another, that you may be healed. The effective, fervent prayer of a righteous man avails much.)!

The Sodomites rejected multiple opportunities to reach for the Living God. These wicked people had once been rescued by Abram **(Genesis 14:14 Now when Abram heard that his brother was taken captive, he armed his three hundred and eighteen trained servants who were born in his own house, and went in pursuit as far as Dan.**

Genesis 14:15 He divided his forces against them by night, and he and his servants attacked them and pursued them as far as Hobah, which is north of Damascus.

Genesis 14:16 So he brought back all the goods, and also brought back his brother Lot and his goods, as well as the women and the people.). The king of Sodom had witnessed Abram worship God with Melchizedek

(Genesis 14:17 And the king of Sodom went out to meet him at the Valley of Shaveh (that is, the King's Valley), after his return from the defeat of Chedorlaomer and the kings who were with him.

Genesis 14:18 Abram and Melchizedek

Then Melchizedek king of Salem brought out bread and wine; he was the priest of God Most High.

Genesis 14:19 And he blessed him and said:

"Blessed be Abram of God Most High,

Possessor of heaven and earth;

Genesis 14:20 And blessed be God Most High,

Who has delivered your enemies into your hand."

And he gave him a tithe of all.).

And they had a righteous man living among them in Lot (although a very weak man of God). In these interactions, they had access to—but still rejected—the Truth.

The destruction of Sodom and Gomorrah reminds us of the ultimate cost of rebellion against God. God sent His own Son to bridge the gap between His holiness and our depravity. On the Cross, Jesus took the weight of all sin—yours and mine—so we could be reconciled to God. Three days after His crucifixion, He rose from the grave and defeated sin and death, once and for all.

Each of us falls short of God's holiness (**Romans 3:23 for all have sinned and fall short of the glory of God,**),

but God made a way by sacrificing His son, Jesus (**Romans 6:23 For the wages of sin is death, but the gift of God is eternal life in Christ Jesus our Lord.**),

to be the propitiation or atonement for our sins. The continued rejection of Christ leads to death and destruction

(Matthew 10:33 But whoever denies Me before men, him I will also deny before My Father who is in heaven.,

Mark 8:38 For whoever is ashamed of Me and My words in this adulterous and sinful generation, of him the Son of Man also will be ashamed when He comes in the glory of His Father with the holy angels."

Matthew 25:31 The Son of Man Will Judge the Nations

"When the Son of Man comes in His glory, and all the holy angels with Him, then He will sit on the throne of His glory.

Matthew 25:32 All the nations will be gathered before Him, and He will separate them one from another, as a shepherd divides his sheep from the goats.

Matthew 25:33 And He will set the sheep on His right hand, but the goats on the left.

Matthew 25:34 Then the King will say to those on His right hand, 'Come, you blessed of My Father, inherit the kingdom prepared for you from the foundation of the world:

Matthew 25:35 for I was hungry and you gave Me food; I was thirsty and you gave Me drink; I was a stranger and you took Me in;

Matthew 25:36 I was naked and you clothed Me; I was sick and you visited Me; I was in prison and you came to Me.'

Matthew 25:37 "Then the righteous will answer Him, saying, 'Lord, when did we see You hungry and feed You, or thirsty and give You drink?

Matthew 25:38 When did we see You a stranger and take You in, or naked and clothe You?

Matthew 25:39 Or when did we see You sick, or in prison, and come to You?'

Matthew 25:40 And the King will answer and say to them, 'Assuredly, I say to you, inasmuch as you did it to one of the least of these My brethren, you did it to Me.'

Matthew 25:41 "Then He will also say to those on the left hand, 'Depart from Me, you cursed, into the everlasting fire prepared for the devil and his angels:

Matthew 25:42 for I was hungry and you gave Me no food; I was thirsty and you gave Me no drink;

Matthew 25:43 I was a stranger and you did not take Me in, naked and you did not clothe Me, sick and in prison and you did not visit Me.'

Matthew 25:44 "Then they also will answer Him, saying, 'Lord, when did we see You hungry or thirsty or a stranger or naked or sick or in prison, and did not minister to You?'

Matthew 25:45 Then He will answer them, saying, 'Assuredly, I say to you, inasmuch as you did not do it to one of the least of these, you did not do it to Me.'

Matthew 25:46 And these will go away into everlasting punishment, but the righteous into eternal life.")

and to a rush of Divine wrath even more terrifying than that experienced in Sodom and Gomorrah.

As we stand beside Abraham and look out over the ruins of Sodom and Gomorrah, we must approach this ancient scene of desolation in humility—and in gratitude for the redemption offered by Jesus' sacrifice. A Holy God demanded justice—payment—for sin, and Jesus, the precious Lamb of God, was the perfect fulfillment of this requirement.

May we turn from the pride and selfishness that leads to destruction and reach for God's life-giving offer of salvation. Then, in fullness of joy, may we invest our lives in the great adventure of loving Jesus and in sharing His love and hope with the world.

The story of Sodom and Gomorrah primarily teaches that unchecked wickedness and a lack of hospitality can lead to severe consequences, serving as a warning against embracing immoral behavior and highlighting the importance of standing against evil, even when surrounded by it; key lessons include: the reality of God's judgment, the need to actively resist sin, the value of righteousness even in a corrupt society, and the potential for God's mercy through individuals like Lot who choose to remain faithful despite their circumstances.

CHAPTER SEVEN

THE REBELLION OF KORAH

The Korah rebellion was a revolt against Moses and Aaron in the Bible, as described in Numbers 16. The rebellion was led by Korah, Dathan, and Abiram, along with 250 other men.

Numbers 16:1-32

Numbers 16:1 Rebellion Against Moses and Aaron

Now Korah the son of Izhar, the son of Kohath, the son of Levi, with Dathan and Abiram the sons of Eliab, and On the son of Peleth, sons of Reuben, took men;

Numbers 16:2 and they rose up before Moses with some of the children of Israel, two hundred and fifty leaders of the congregation, representatives of the congregation, men of renown.

Numbers 16:3 They gathered together against Moses and Aaron, and said to them, "You take too much upon yourselves, for all the congregation is holy, every one of them, and the Lord is among them. Why then do you exalt yourselves above the assembly of the Lord?"

Numbers 16:4 So when Moses heard it, he fell on his face;

Numbers 16:5 and he spoke to Korah and all his company, saying, "Tomorrow morning the Lord will show who is His and who is holy, and will cause him to come near to Him. That one whom He chooses He will cause to come near to Him.

Numbers 16:6 Do this: Take censers, Korah and all your company;

Numbers 16:7 put fire in them and put incense in them before the Lord tomorrow, and it shall be that the man whom the Lord chooses is the holy one. You take too much upon yourselves, you sons of Levi!"

Numbers 16:8 Then Moses said to Korah, "Hear now, you sons of Levi:

Numbers 16:9 Is it a small thing to you that the God of Israel has separated you from the congregation of Israel, to bring you near to Himself, to do the work of the tabernacle of the Lord, and to stand before the congregation to serve them;

Numbers 16:10 and that He has brought you near to Himself, you and all your brethren, the sons of Levi, with you? And are you seeking the priesthood also?

Numbers 16:11 Therefore you and all your company are gathered together against the Lord. And what is Aaron that you complain against him?"

Numbers 16:12 And Moses sent to call Dathan and Abiram the sons of Eliab, but they said, "We will not come up!

Numbers 16:13 Is it a small thing that you have brought us up out of a land flowing with milk and honey, to kill us in the wilderness, that you should keep acting like a prince over us?

Numbers 16:14 Moreover you have not brought us into a land flowing with milk and honey, nor given us inheritance of fields and vineyards. Will you put out the eyes of these men? We will not come up!"

Numbers 16:15 Then Moses was very angry, and said to the Lord, "Do not respect their offering. I have not taken one donkey from them, nor have I hurt one of them."

Numbers 16:16 And Moses said to Korah, "Tomorrow, you and all your company be present before the Lord—you and they, as well as Aaron.

Numbers 16:17 Let each take his censer and put incense in it, and each of you bring his censer before the Lord, two hundred and fifty censers; both you and Aaron, each with his censer."

Numbers 16:18 So every man took his censer, put fire in it, laid incense on it, and stood at the door of the tabernacle of meeting with Moses and Aaron.

Numbers 16:19 And Korah gathered all the congregation against them at the door of the tabernacle of meeting. Then the glory of the Lord appeared to all the congregation.

Numbers 16:20 And the Lord spoke to Moses and Aaron, saying,

Numbers 16:21 "Separate yourselves from among this congregation, that I may consume them in a moment."

Numbers 16:22 Then they fell on their faces, and said, "O God, the God of the spirits of all flesh, shall one man sin, and You be angry with all the congregation?"

Numbers 16:23 So the Lord spoke to Moses, saying,

Numbers 16:24 "Speak to the congregation, saying, 'Get away from the tents of Korah, Dathan, and Abiram.'"

Numbers 16:25 Then Moses rose and went to Dathan and Abiram, and the elders of Israel followed him.

Numbers 16:26 And he spoke to the congregation, saying, "Depart now from the tents of these wicked men! Touch nothing of theirs, lest you be consumed in all their sins."

Numbers 16:27 So they got away from around the tents of Korah, Dathan, and Abiram; and Dathan and Abiram came out and stood at the door of their tents, with their wives, their sons, and their little children.

Numbers 16:28 And Moses said: "By this you shall know that the Lord has sent me to do all these works, for I have not done them of my own will.

Numbers 16:29 If these men die naturally like all men, or if they are visited by the common fate of all men, then the Lord has not sent me.

Numbers 16:30 But if the Lord creates a new thing, and the earth opens its mouth and swallows them up with all that belongs to them, and they go down alive into the pit, then you will understand that these men have rejected the Lord."

Numbers 16:31 Now it came to pass, as he finished speaking all these words, that the ground split apart under them,

Numbers 16:32 and the earth opened its mouth and swallowed them up, with their households and all the men with Korah, with all their goods.

Numbers 16:33 So they and all those with them went down alive into the pit; the earth closed over them, and they perished from among the assembly.

Numbers 16:34 Then all Israel who were around them fled at their cry, for they said, "Lest the earth swallow us up also!"

Numbers 16:35 And a fire came out from the Lord and consumed the two hundred and fifty men who were offering incense.

Obviously, Korah thought that he could do a better job leading the people than Moses was doing. But by leading this revolt against God's divinely appointed leaders, Korah was actually revolting against God (Numbers 16:11). Moses proposed a test to prove the source of his authority. Korah and his followers did not pass the test, and God opened up the earth and swallowed the rebels, their families, and all their possessions. Furthermore, "fire came out from the LORD" and consumed the other 250 men who were party to Korah's rebellion. The rest of the Israelites were terrified and fled (Numbers 16:31-35).

The following day, instead of being convinced that God had vindicated Moses and Aaron, the congregation began complaining that they had "killed the LORD's people." For this act of rebellion, God threatened to destroy the whole congregation and sent a plague among them. However, Moses and Aaron interceded for the rebels and averted a complete catastrophe. In the end, 14,700 Israelites had died (Numbers 16:41-50).

Some 1,500 years later, Jude records a strong warning about such men who come into the church as false teachers, arrogating to themselves the authority of God and His Word: "Woe to them! For they walked in the way of Cain and abandoned themselves for the sake of gain to

Balaam's error and perished in Korah's rebellion" (**Jude 1:11 Woe to them! For they have gone in the way of Cain, have run greedily in the error of Balaam for profit, and perished in the rebellion of Korah.**)

The characteristics of false teachers within the church include pride, selfishness, jealousy, greed, lust for power, and disregard for the will of God. Just like Korah, today's false teachers disregard God's plan and are insubordinate to God's appointed authorities. Their end will be the same as Korah's. Thus the warning: "Woe to them!"

To lead His people Israel, God had selected men of His own choosing. God had no interest in holding a popularity contest, collecting résumés, or letting someone appoint himself to the position of prophet, priest, or leader. Korah's problem was not that he was unqualified, humanly speaking, for the position, but that he was arrogant, stiff-necked, and self-promoting. Korah, attempting to install himself as the leader, ironically claims that Moses "set [himself] above the LORD's assembly." It's a classic case of the guilty person accusing someone else of his own misdeed. But God did not call Korah; He called Moses (Exodus 3-4). God calls whom He chooses and equips them for service.

God's true leaders, the elders and pastors of the church who shepherd the flock with humility and care, have an accurate understanding of the Scriptures (see **. Malachi 3:18 Then you shall again discern Between the righteous and the wicked, Between one who serves God And one who does not serve Him.;**

Romans 12:2 And do not be conformed to this world, but be transformed by the renewing of your mind, that you may prove what is that good and acceptable and perfect will of God.

Ephesians 5:10 finding out what is acceptable to the Lord.

Ephesians 5:11 And have no fellowship with the unfruitful works of darkness, but rather expose them.).

Such men submit themselves in humble adoration of Christ and His lordship (see Matthew **16:16 Simon Peter answered and said, "You are the Christ, the Son of the living God.";**

Colossians 2:9 For in Him dwells all the fullness of the Godhead bodily;

1 Timothy 3:16 And without controversy great is the mystery of godliness:

God was manifested in the flesh, Justified in the Spirit, Seen by angels,

Preached among the Gentiles, Believed on in the world,Received up in glory.).

They recognize the truth of Jesus' proclamation, "I am the way, and the truth, and the life. No one comes to the Father except through me" (John 14:6 Jesus said to him, "I am the way, the truth, and the life. No one comes to the Father except through Me.). Most importantly, the true leaders of the church are called by God to their office. False teachers, on the other hand, are "wolves in sheep's clothing" (Matthew 7:15 You Will Know Them by Their Fruits

"Beware of false prophets, who come to you in sheep's clothing, but inwardly they are ravenous wolves.; .

The Acts 20:29 For I know this, that after my departure savage wolves will come in among you, not sparing the flock.) who choose the fate of Korah over the life of Christ.

To overcome a "Korah's Rebellion"-like situation, which represents a rebellion against established leadership fueled by envy and discontent, one should prioritize open communication, addressing concerns directly, upholding God-ordained authority, remaining humble, and allowing God to judge the situation rather than taking personal vengeance; essentially, focusing on resolving conflict peacefully and with a spirit of unity, while respecting the designated leaders and their roles.

Key points to remember from the story of Korah:

- Address concerns directly:

Leaders should not shy away from confronting issues raised by those rebelling, trying to understand their grievances and addressing them openly.

- Maintain humility:

Leaders should not react with pride or anger, but instead demonstrate humility and a willingness to listen to opposing viewpoints.

- Uphold God-ordained authority:

Remind people of the established leadership structure and the importance of respecting the authority God has placed in position.

- Seek unity and reconciliation:

Focus on bringing the group together and finding common ground rather than escalating conflict.

- Leave judgement to God:

Instead of taking personal revenge, trust that God will ultimately judge the situation and those involved.

How to apply these principles in a modern context:

In a workplace:

If a team member is expressing discontent with a project or leadership decisions, address the concerns directly, listen actively, and work together to find solutions that benefit the whole team.

In a community:

If disagreements arise within a group, encourage open dialogue, seek common ground, and work towards resolving issues through collaboration and respect for different perspectives.

In personal relationships:

If a conflict arises with a friend or family member, try to understand their perspective, communicate openly, and seek reconciliation without resorting to personal attacks.

CHAPTER EIGHT

REBELLION OF THE CHILDREN OF ISRAEL

The Israelites rebelled against God by breaking the Mosaic covenant and worshipping other gods. This rebellion is described in the Bible in books such as Exodus, Ezekiel, and Numbers.

Seven Rebellions

Once the people leave Mt. Sinai in Numbers 10, things go terribly wrong. Every story to follow begins with a moment of Israelite insurrection: the people complain or rebel or grumble.

1."And the people complained about their hardships." (**Numbers 11:1 The People Complain**

Now when the people complained, it displeased the Lord; for the Lord heard it, and His anger was aroused. So the fire of the Lord burned among them, and consumed some in the outskirts of the camp.) "And the rabble among them had greedy desires... and said 'Who will give us meat?!'" (**Numbers 11:4 Now the mixed multitude who were among them yielded to intense craving; so the children of Israel also wept again and said: "Who will give us meat to eat?)**

2."And Miriam and Aaron spoke against Moses." (**Numbers 12:1 Dissension of Aaron and Miriam**

Then Miriam and Aaron spoke against Moses because of the Ethiopian woman whom he had married; for he had married an Ethiopian woman.

3."And all the community raised their voice... and grumbled against Moses and Aaron." (**Numbers 14:1 Israel Refuses to Enter Canaan**

So all the congregation lifted up their voices and cried, and the people wept that night.

Numbers 14:2 And all the children of Israel complained against Moses and Aaron, and the whole congregation said to them, "If only we had died in the land of Egypt! Or if only we had died in this wilderness!)

4."And Korah... with Nathan and Abiram... with two hundred and fifty leaders of the community... rose up against Moses." (**Numbers 16:1 Rebellion Against Moses and Aaron**

Now Korah the son of Izhar, the son of Kohath, the son of Levi, with Dathan and Abiram the sons of Eliab, and On the son of Peleth, sons of Reuben, took men;

Numbers 16:2 and they rose up before Moses with some of the children of Israel, two hundred and fifty leaders of the congregation, representatives of the congregation, men of renown.

Numbers 16:3 They gathered together against Moses and Aaron, and said to them, "You take too much upon yourselves, for all the congregation is holy, every one of them, and the Lord is among them. Why then do you exalt yourselves above the assembly of the Lord?")

5."And the entire community grumbled against Moses and Aaron." (**Numbers 16:41 Complaints of the People**

On the next day all the congregation of the children of Israel complained against Moses and Aaron, saying, "You have killed the people of the Lord.")

6."And the people quarreled with Moses." (**Numbers 20:3 And the people contended with Moses and spoke, saying: "If only we had died when our brethren died before the Lord!)**

7."And the people spoke against God and Moses." (**Numbers 21:5 And the people spoke against God and against Moses: "Why have you brought us up out of Egypt to die in the wilderness? For there is no food and no water, and our soul loathes this worthless bread.")**

Moses begins a dialogue with God, who is angry at the people's rebellion and threatens to destroy them. Moses pleads and intercedes on their behalf, wanting to protect God's reputation among the nations. He knows that God has every right to punish but asks for forgiveness.

CHAPTER NINE

MOSES REBELLION

According to the Bible, Moses rebelled against God by striking a rock instead of speaking to it, as God had instructed. This incident occurred at the Rock of Meribah while the Israelites were wandering in the wilderness.

Moses' harsh words toward the Israelites reveal his emotions in this moment; he classifies Israel as "rebels" rather than the chosen people, and his rhetorical question seems to imply that he does not view Israel as worthy of God's grace any longer. This is the real failure of Moses in this moment: he's lost his faith in God to fulfill His promises to these people. Israel is a nation of rebels outside of grace, outside of God's ability to make a great nation, outside of the promises that God has given. It seems nearly forty years of dealing with this people has finally broken Moses, and he is so overwhelmed in this moment that he has lost faith. From God's perspective, Moses has lost faith in the Lord to overcome Israel's faithlessness. Moses has not believed in God, and has not treated Yahweh as the Holy God who is able to overcome the weakness of His people. Indeed, this is exactly what Numbers 20:12 says was Moses' sin! He (and Aaron!) did not believe God and did not treat Yahweh as holy in that moment. God did offer Moses the opportunity to intercede for the people (and thus broke the pattern) because He knew that Moses did not have faith in Him.

Numbers 20:8

Take the rod; and you and your brother Aaron assemble the congregation and speak to the rock before their eyes, that it may yield its water. You shall thus bring forth water for them out of the rock and let the congregation and their beasts drink. Instead of speaking to the rock, Moses strikes it (as he did in Exodus 17), but it still works and produces water.

Not only does Moses do something other than what God told him to do, he suggests that he and Aaron are responsible for producing the water (Num. 20:10). While the incident may seem relatively small, the narrator is highlighting for us that Moses is standing in the tradition of Adam and Eve (and every chosen one ever since) who failed to do what God said. God's word is life for humanity and to ignore it brings death.

The way that Yahweh responds to Moses reveals that Moses' choice was intentional rebellion, and Yahweh forbids them from entering the promised land (Num. 20:12). The point of this story is not for us to walk on eggshells with Yahweh because he might punish our smallest mistake. Rather, it's about Moses' intentional choice to ignore God's word.

Remember, Moses is not an average person. He's God's chosen representative.

The closer you are to Yahweh (both metaphorically and, in Moses' and Aaron's case, literally), the higher the stakes of responsibility.

Moses' rebellion against God had several consequences, including being denied entry to the Promised Land, and the Israelites being punished for their disobedience.

Moses' punishment

- Denied entry to the Promised Land

Moses was punished for his disobedience, pride, and misrepresenting Christ's sacrifice.

- Allowed to see the Promised Land

God showed Moses the Promised Land before his death, but Moses was not allowed to enter.

Personal Assessment

As you continue reading this book ,take time now and assess yourself ,ask the LORD to intervene and check the status of your heart .

Note down all the instances of rebellion in your life ,be honest

Now it's time to Repent .

If you have been rebellious, then stop! Forsake your rebellion and turn to the Lord. Repent of thy ways, that ye shall receive mercy. Rebellion is an open door to demonic spirits in a person's life. God's Word warns us that rebellion darkens your spiritual eyesight (discernment), and it deafens your ears to hear God's voice.

CHAPTER TEN

REBELLION DURING NOAHS TIME

There were rebellions against God during Noah's time, including the building of the Tower of Babel and the actions of the Nephilim.

The Tower of Babel

Noah's descendants rebelled against God by building the Tower of Babel after the flood.

When God blessed Noah and his sons after the global flood, he told them to "be fruitful and multiply and fill the earth" (Genesis 9:1). But only about a century later, we see that man seems to have no interest in obeying the command to fill the earth.

Now the whole earth had one language and the same words. And as people migrated from the east, they found a plain in the land of Shinar and settled there. And they said to one another, "Come, let us make bricks, and burn them thoroughly." And they had brick for stone, and bitumen for mortar. Then they said, "Come, let us build ourselves a city and a tower with its top in the heavens, and let us make a name for ourselves, lest we be dispersed over the face of the whole earth." (Genesis 11:1–4)

Fueled by pride, the people preferred to "make a name" for themselves and build a city with a high tower, enabling them to remain together in defiance of God's command. The proposed construction began. Composed of brick and mortar, this city was intended to be permanent and impressive—a fortress against any natural or supernatural attempt to disperse mankind throughout the earth.

But God was neither unaware of their actions nor powerless against their plans. In his mercy, he intervened—not by destruction as he had during the flood, nor by directly driving them out to be fugitives and wanderers (as in the record of Cain's judgment; see Genesis 4:12). Instead, God divided their single language into multiple language families.

And the Lord came down to see the city and the tower, which the children of man had built. And the Lord said, "Behold, they are one people, and they have all one language, and this is only the beginning of what they will do. And nothing that they propose to do will now be impossible for them. Come, let us go down and there confuse their language, so that they may not understand one another's speech." (Genesis 11:5–7)

For the first time in earth's history, there was a language barrier. Without a common language, the people who had been so adamant about staying together were now unable to even understand each other. Construction of the city ceased—whether because they lost interest in the city due to the futility of attempting to coordinate such a massive project without a means of communication (not to mention losing the appeal of living together as one people) or because they recognized God's judgment and feared a worse sentence should they attempt to continue in their rebellion.

Whatever the case, God's judgment was effective. The attempted "one-world kingdom" fractured. Smaller groups formed from those sharing each of the new languages, and people began scattering from the city.

So the Lord dispersed them from there over the face of all the earth, and they left off building the city. Therefore its name was called Babel, because there the Lord confused the language of all the earth. And from there the Lord dispersed them over the face of all the earth. (Genesis 11:8–9)

The Nephilim

In Genesis 6, the Nephilim were mysterious characters who were the result of a rebellion between angels and humans.

The angels lusted after human women and intermarried with them, which led to the birth of giants.

The Nephilim were a part of the rebellion that led to the corruption of the human race.

God did not allow the human race to stay in this rebellious place forever. This means there is a point of no return in our rejection of God. God will not woo us forever; there is a point where He will say "no more."

Genesis 6:6 says that "The LORD regretted that he had made human beings on the earth, and his heart was deeply troubled." And, in response, God determined to destroy all life on the earth. It would be easy to read this and see a God who was caught off guard by how sinful humanity had become. A God who became so angry that he decided to wipe out the whole mess and start over again.

Just like in Noah's time, our world is filled with violence, corruption, and immorality. People have become selfish, greedy, and cruel, with no regard for God or His laws. As 2 Timothy 3:1-5 warns, "But mark this: There will be terrible times in the last days. People will be lovers of themselves, lovers of money, boastful, proud, abusive, disobedient to their parents, ungrateful, unholy, without love, unforgiving, slanderous, without self-control, brutal, not lovers of the good, treacherous, rash, conceited, lovers of pleasure rather than lovers of God."

Furthermore, just as God sent a flood to destroy the wickedness of humanity in Noah's time (Genesis 6:17), He will soon send judgment upon the world for its sins. As Jesus said in Luke 17:26-27, "Just as it was in the days of Noah, so also will it be in the days of the Son of Man. People were eating, drinking, marrying and being given in marriage up to the day Noah entered the ark. Then the flood came and destroyed them all."

However, just as Noah and his family were saved from the flood, those who put their trust in God and obey His commands will be saved from the coming judgment. As 1 Peter 3:20-21 says, "God waited patiently in the days of Noah while the ark was being built. In it only a few people, eight in all, were saved through water, and this water symbolizes baptism that now saves you also—not the removal of dirt from the body but the pledge of a clear conscience toward God."

CHAPTER ELEVEN

ABSALOMS REBELLION

Absalom's rebellion was a revolt against King David by his son Absalom. The rebellion is described in the Bible in 2 Samuel 13–18.

Absalom's story is one of pride and greed, about a man who tried to overthrow the plan of God. His ambition and rebellion against his father not only led to his own demise but also brought turmoil to the kingdom of Israel. Interestingly, Absalom was known for his extraordinary good looks and luxurious hair, which he cut only once a year; this very hair ultimately contributed to his death.

The wheels started to come off the train when David's son Amnon raped his half-sister, Tamar. Tamar's brother, Absalom (Amnon's half-brother), was enraged by his brother's sin and eventually had Amnon killed (2 Samuel 13).

This was a low blow for David, but the hits had just started coming. Absalom fled to live with his grandparents. During that long season of waiting, a bitter root started to grow in Absalom's heart. Though his father eventually welcomed him home with a kiss, Absalom began to plot a coup to take the throne. He launched a PR campaign, tricked 200 men into joining his cause, recruited David's advisers, amassed an army, and prepared to march on to Jerusalem.

The same David who had been promised a kingdom that would last forever put on a disguise and ran for his life.

Though the battle cost him mightily—20,000 casualties, including his own son—David kept his throne, and God kept His promises. Yes, David was highly favored by God, but that didn't vaccinate him from hard work and heartbreak

The Result of Absalom's Rebellion

Absalom continues to lead Israel against David but eventually loses the battle to his father. He is killed by Joab at the time when he was caught in a tree. This shows another example that pride goes before destruction (Proverbs 16:18). He wanted to be greater than his father and led an army, but was defeated.

Though it may seem like Absalom had a right to be angry, we must remember that everything he did was due to pride and bitterness towards his father. Because of these two factors, he lost everything including his life by trying to overthrow his father. There are so many lessons from this narrative but bottom line is – don't be an Absalom!

Absalom imitated his father's weaknesses instead of his strengths. He allowed selfishness to rule him, instead of God's law. When he tried to oppose God's plan and unseat the rightful king, destruction came upon him.

Key Bible Verses

2 Samuel 15:10

Then Absalom sent secret messengers throughout the tribes of Israel to say, "As soon as you hear the sound of the trumpets, then say, 'Absalom is king in Hebron.'" (NIV)

2 Samuel 18:33

The king was shaken. He went up to the room over the gateway and wept. As he went, he said: "O my son Absalom! My son, my son Absalom! If only I had died instead of you—O Absalom, my son, my son!" (NIV)

CHAPTER TWELVE

THE SPIRIT OF REBELLION IN TODAYS WORLD AND THE CONSEQUENCES OF THE SPIRIT OF REBELLION

In today's world, the "spirit of rebellion" manifests as a widespread attitude of resistance towards established authority, often seen in movements challenging social norms, political structures, and traditional power dynamics, fueled by a desire for individual autonomy, questioning of the status quo, and sometimes even outright defiance against perceived injustices, which can play out in various forms from peaceful protests to online activism to more radical actions depending on the context.

A person with a rebellious spirit lives by his/her own rules, values, morals, worldly standards, and principles; instead of what has been established by God. They willfully walk in disobedience, ignoring God's voice and His warnings. A person with a rebellious spirit believes they are in control....even if those around them can see the trainwreck coming miles ahead. They have this attitude of, "I am going to do, say, and be who I want to be, regardless of what others say or think." They try to justify their wrongdoings by pointing out the wrongdoings of others. They will not take accountability for their actions but will make excuses for them.

Rebellion undermines authority. Possessing this type of spirit can cause a person to rebel against parents, spouses, government officials, law enforcement, employers, pastors, and other church leaders, to satisfy their flesh or carry out their own agendas. (If something is morally or ethically wrong, then, yes, rebellion is justified.)

"Woe to the rebellious children, saith the Lord, that take counsel, but not of me; and that cover with a covering, but not of my spirit, that they may add sin to sin." Isaiah 30:1 KJV

The underlying theme of these times is to deny yourself nothing. However, to be a true follower of Christ, you must deny yourself. Jesus says to his disciples in Luke 9:23, **"... if any man will come after me, let him deny himself, and take up his cross daily and follow me."**

When in rebellion, you will always make allowances for what soothes your flesh or give you relief. When someone is comfortable in their sin, wants to stay in or hold onto sin, they always find a way to justify it....to make it seem normal and right.

We must remember that the enemy is a master deceiver. There will be times when we fall victim to his traps, tricks, and schemes unknowingly and make honest mistakes. Once we recognize it, our conviction should automatically cause us to repent.

Then on the other side of that, there are times when we know or are conscious of our decision, we know it is wrong, we hear God's voice, and still choose to do it anyway in direct rebellion....choosing not to submit or repent in opposition to God. This is never a good or wise choice. There is no peace where there is rebellion. It can and it will only end in destruction or death....physically or spiritually.

"Therefore, to him, that knoweth to do good, and doeth it not, to him it is sin." James 4:17 KJV

We all have dealt with or are currently dealing with this spirit of rebellion in some form or aspect of our lives....even those who profess to be believers or Christians. As stated previously, a rebellious spirit can and will affect our hearts, our homes, and our relationships with family and friends, and destroy marriages and even churches.

Truthfully, ANY sin can separate us from God. ALL sin is deceptive and destructive and has dire consequences. When we don't kill the sin, it will set up strongholds and continue to get passed down through generations, if not cut off at the root.

"God setteth the solitary in families: he bringeth out those which are bound with chains: but the rebellious dwell in a dry land." Psalms 68:6 KJV

THE SPIRIT OF REBELLION

Pray for strength to resist. Pray for discernment to know God's voice from that of the god of this world, Satan. Pray for humility. Cover yourself and your loved ones in prayer. We must be cognizant of what we feed our flesh and what we feed our spirit daily. What is on the inside will show up or manifest on the outside.

~ To be led by Him, we must be fed by Him!

In Christian life today, the "spirit of rebellion" can manifest in various forms, including: disregarding biblical teachings, prioritizing personal desires over God's will, criticizing church leadership without valid reason, actively resisting authority figures, stubbornness in sin, neglecting spiritual disciplines, and a general attitude of self-sufficiency, where individuals believe they can live life without relying on God; essentially, any behavior that actively opposes or disregards God's commands and guidance.

Specific examples of this spirit of rebellion might include:

- Ignoring church doctrine:

Choosing to not follow established Christian beliefs or practices, even when they are clearly outlined in scripture.

- Consistently missing church services:

Deliberately skipping church gatherings without a valid reason, demonstrating a lack of commitment to community worship.

- Complaining about leadership without seeking solutions:

Criticizing church leaders or policies without attempting to engage in constructive dialogue or seek change through proper channels.

- Refusing to submit to spiritual authority:

Rejecting guidance from pastors or mentors, even when it aligns with biblical teachings.

- Justifying sinful behavior:

Rationalizing personal actions that go against Christian values, minimizing the severity of one's choices.

- Pride and arrogance:

Believing oneself to be above accountability or correction, displaying a self-centered attitude.

- Disrespecting family members:

Failing to honor parents or other family leaders, exhibiting rebellious behavior within the household.

- Actively promoting opposing views:

Publicly advocating against Christian teachings or values, especially when it undermines the community.

People today believe they can run away from God, resist his claim on their lives, do their own thing and then ask God to bless them. They believe they can sin and escape the consequences of that sin. They are wrong. A price must be paid for rebelling against God

Consequences of The Spirit of Rebellion

It is dangerous to rebel against the will and the Word of God and to turn away from His path. Psalm 107 describes the fate of people who did.

Psalms 107:10 Those who sat in darkness and in the shadow of death,

Bound in affliction and irons—

Psalms 107:11 Because they rebelled against the words of God,

And despised the counsel of the Most High,

Psalms 107:12 Therefore He brought down their heart with labor;

They fell down, and there was none to help.

Psalms 107:13 Then they cried out to the Lord in their trouble,

And He saved them out of their distresses.

Psalms 107:14 He brought them out of darkness and the shadow of death,

And broke their chains in pieces.

This is the terrible and painful plight of all who rebel against God's will and Word—darkness, death and despair. Instead of being on that wonderful road that leads to glory, they are down in the dungeon in darkness and in bondage, under the shadow of death.

People say, "I want to do my own thing. I want to do it my way." They shouldn't. The greatest judgment God might bring to our lives is to let us have our own way.

Paul wrote that God gave mankind over to uncleanness, vile passions and a debased mind (Rom. 1:18-32

Romans 1:18 God's Wrath on Unrighteousness

For the wrath of God is revealed from heaven against all ungodliness and unrighteousness of men, who suppress the truth in unrighteousness,

Romans 1:19 because what may be known of God is manifest in them, for God has shown it to them.

Romans 1:20 For since the creation of the world His invisible attributes are clearly seen, being understood by the things that are made, even His eternal power and Godhead, so that they are without excuse,

Romans 1:21 because, although they knew God, they did not glorify Him as God, nor were thankful, but became futile in their thoughts, and their foolish hearts were darkened.

Romans 1:22 Professing to be wise, they became fools,

Romans 1:23 and changed the glory of the incorruptible God into an image made like corruptible man—and birds and four-footed animals and creeping things.

Romans 1:24 Therefore God also gave them up to uncleanness, in the lusts of their hearts, to dishonor their bodies among themselves,

Romans 1:25 who exchanged the truth of God for the lie, and worshiped and served the creature rather than the Creator, who is blessed forever. Amen.

Romans 1:26 For this reason God gave them up to vile passions. For even their women exchanged the natural use for what is against nature.

Romans 1:27 Likewise also the men, leaving the natural use of the woman, burned in their lust for one another, men with men committing what is shameful, and receiving in themselves the penalty of their error which was due.

Romans 1:28 And even as they did not like to retain God in their knowledge, God gave them over to a debased mind, to do those things which are not fitting;

Romans 1:29 being filled with all unrighteousness, sexual immorality, wickedness, covetousness, maliciousness; full of envy, murder, strife, deceit, evil-mindedness; they are whisperers,

Romans 1:30 backbiters, haters of God, violent, proud, boasters, inventors of evil things, disobedient to parents,

Romans 1:31 undiscerning, untrustworthy, unloving, unforgiving, unmerciful;

Romans 1:32 who, knowing the righteous judgment of God, that those who practice such things are deserving of death, not only do the same but also approve of those who practice them.).

God says to those who rebel against Him, "Do you want to go in that direction? All right, I won't stop you, but neither will I change the consequences."

The people described in Psalm 107 who rebelled against God's Word ended up in darkness and death, in the dungeon of defeat and despair.

But they cried out to God, and He delivered them.

It's never too late for God's mercy. You can cry out to Him just as these people did

Rebellion brings you down from a great height. When your will is elevated, pride is high, no matter what height you have gained in life, rebellion will result in God bringing you down. In Isaiah 14:12-15, when Satan decided that what he wanted was above God's order of things, God vowed to bring him down. What height have you fallen from?

Rebellion cuts you off from Kingdom privileges. In Ezekiel 28:12-15 the human king of Tyre (also describing Satan) lost the privileges he previously had in the kingdom and it all ceased on the day of his rebellion. Have you felt cut off from God, from His presence, from being used by Him? Cut off from all benefits of a relationship with Him

Rebellion leads one into dryness. Psalm 68:6 "The rebellious dwell in dry land..." Dry of faith, dry of passion, dry in prayer, in finances, in relationships, in vision. When we are in a dry land, everything about us becomes dry. It becomes a spiritual desert, and you start to thirst for something different.

Rebellion shuts one's spiritual eyes and ears. In Ezekiel 12:2(MSG) "God's Message came to me: "Son of man, you're living with a bunch of rebellious people. They have eyes but don't see a thing, they have ears but don't hear a thing. They're rebels all. "

Rebellion makes it hard to see God's way, makes it hard to see things in the spiritual realm, it makes it hard to hear his voice and direction. We lack discernment and we lack confidence in the Spirit. When our spiritual senses are lost, we are close to destruction. As king

Zedekiah was, the last King of Israel, when Ezekiel gave him this warning. Soon they would be taken into captivity just as Ezekiel had warned him, but he was unable to hear or see God.

Rebellion makes the Holy Spirit your enemy. In Isaiah 63:10 it clearly states that rebellion grieves the Holy Spirit and where He is supposed to be our helper and comforter, He now encounters a hardened heart that will not submit to His direction. We set Him up as our enemy.

CHAPTER THIRTEEN

OVERCOMING THE SPIRIT OF REBELLION

To overcome the spirit of rebellion in a Christian life, focus on actively submitting your will to God through prayer, deep study of scripture, seeking guidance from spiritual leaders, identifying the root causes of your rebellious tendencies, and actively choosing obedience even when it's difficult, all while relying on the Holy Spirit to empower you to resist temptation and live in alignment with God's will.

Key steps:

- Deepen your relationship with God:

Spend dedicated time in prayer and Bible study to understand God's commands and develop a closer connection with Him.

- Repentance and confession:

Acknowledge your rebellious thoughts and actions, and actively repent to God, asking for forgiveness and renewal.

- Submit your will to God:

Intentionally choose to obey God's instructions, even when they are challenging, and surrender your own desires to His plan.

- Seek guidance from leaders:

Consult with pastors, mentors, or trusted Christian friends for advice and support in overcoming rebellious tendencies.

- Identify root causes:

Examine your life to identify potential triggers for rebellion, such as pride, fear, or past hurts, and address them with the help of God.

- Practice gratitude:

Focus on thanking God for His blessings and grace to help you resist the temptation to rebel.

- Community involvement:

Actively participate in a supportive Christian community where you can be encouraged and held accountable.

Biblical principles to remember:

✓"Submit yourselves, then, to God. Resist the devil, and he will flee from you." (James 4:7)

✓"Do not be conformed to this world, but be transformed by the renewal of your mind, that by testing you may discern what is the will of God, what is good and acceptable and perfect." (Romans 12:2)

✓"For rebellion is as the sin of divination, and stubbornness is as iniquity and idolatry." (1 Samuel 15:23)

We just need to spend a lot of time with Him, learn to trust Him completely, and submit our will to Him. As you do these things, the Holy Spirit will faithfully lead you out of trouble and into the life that Jesus died to give you—a life of righteousness, peace and joy in the Holy Spirit!

CHAPTER FOURTEEN

CONCLUSION

It's very clear that the spirit of rebellion is deadly and destructive that's why it's ultimate end is death(execution).

The spirit of rebellion" refers to a mindset or attitude characterized by defiance, disobedience, and resistance to authority, often associated with a strong desire to go against established rules or norms, essentially saying "I will not be controlled" and prioritizing one's own will over higher power or leadership; in a religious context, it can be seen as actively opposing God's will.

There are many other instances in the Bible where people were very rebellious either to the authority and to God .In our today's world ,it looks fashionable when one is considered a rebel.Its very sad to see rebels celebrated in the name of they are couragcous and they speak their own mind.We have read about the end of the so celebrated rebels ,they died miserable .

This spirit is characterized by arrogance, anger, and disobedience, leading us to resist God's guidance and wisdom. - Lucifer, once a beautiful and powerful angel, fell from heaven due to his pride and rebellion (Isaiah 14:12-15).

We serve a very merciful God in heaven ,who gives us the chance to repent so that we can walk righteously .Let's all take advantage of the grace God has given us to make things right .Apostle Paul is our example of one man who accepted the chance God gave him of repentance ,and he was transformed from a rebellious church persecutor to a powerful Apostle of God.Today we talk about Apostle Pauls Epistles to different churches .

So while you have the light ,work on,while you have the grace fight on and resist the spirit of rebellion.

I believe now you understand the consequences of the spirit of rebellion ,how you can detect it and more importantly how you can overcome it.

You may notice it in your friends or family ,kindly have a conversation with them,pray for them and help them walk the journey to overcome this deadily evil spirit.Do not be harsh on them ,allow them to walk the journey of deliverance and together we will grow together stronger unified in Christ.

THE SPIRIT OF REBELLION

God withholds blessing from those that are rebellious.

Repent and acknowledge that your attitude is wrong. Stop all things and all associations that are contributing to your rebellion. Weed out doubt and unbelief. Humble yourself and place yourself under God's authority, embrace His will and purpose for your life. Get rid of your excuses for your rebellion and pray that you will not be tempted to go back. Ask Holy Spirit to help you to obey.

Let's Pray

Lord the more I reflect on the effects of rebellion the more I have to admit that it has been the state of my heart.

I confess that I rebel against Your will and purpose for my life and instead are determined to have my way and will.

I have been so focused on what I want, that I have not considered what You want. I recognise that rebellion has led to sinful attitudes in my heart, and I have questioned Your heart and Your purposes for my life.

Please forgive me Lord and release me from this spirit of rebellion in me. Release me from thoughts that lie about You.

Release me from an attitude that feels You owe me. Lord, I have been wrong. Wash my heart, my mind, my attitudes to life.

Clean out my pride and help me to have a will that says; "Your will be done in my life Lord."

AMEN

CHAPTER FIFTEEN

BIBLICAL REFERENCES ON REBELLION

- Joshua 22:22 "The Lord God of gods, the Lord God of gods, He knows, and let Israel itself know—if it is in rebellion, or if in treachery against the Lord, do not save us this day.
- 1 Samuel 15:23 For rebellion is as the sin of witchcraft, And stubbornness is as iniquity and idolatry. Because you have rejected the word of the Lord, He also has rejected you from being king."
- 2 Samuel 23:6 But the sons of rebellion shall all be as thorns thrust away, Because they cannot be taken with hands.
- Proverbs 17:11 An evil man seeks only rebellion; Therefore a cruel messenger will be sent against him.
- Jeremiah 28:16 Therefore thus says the Lord: 'Behold, I will cast you from the face of the earth. This year you shall die, because you have taught rebellion against the Lord.'"
- 1 Samuel 12:15 However, if you do not obey the voice of the Lord, but rebel against the commandment of the Lord, then the hand of the Lord will be against you, as it was against your fathers.
- Proverbs 7:11 She was loud and rebellious, Her feet would not stay at home.
- Isaiah 1:20 But if you refuse and rebel, You shall be devoured by the sword"; For the mouth of the Lord has spoken.
- Isaiah 63:10 But they rebelled and grieved His Holy Spirit; So He turned Himself against them as an enemy, And He fought against them.
- Psalms 68:6, "...the rebellious dwell in a dry land.
- Proverbs 20:20, "Whoso curseth his father or his mother, his lamp shall be put out in obscure darkness."

- Psalms 78:8, "And might not be as their fathers, a stubborn and rebellious generation; a generation that set not their heart aright, and whose spirit was not steadfast with God."
- Ezekiel 3:26, "And I will make thy tongue cleave to the roof of thy mouth, that thou shalt be dumb, and shalt not be to them a reprover: for they are a rebellious house."
- Ezekiel 12:2, "Son of man, thou dwellest in the midst of a rebellious house, which have eyes to see, and see not; they have ears to hear, and hear not: for they are a rebellious house."
- 2 Corinthians 4:4, "In whom the god of this world hath blinded the minds of them which believe not, lest the light of the glorious gospel of Christ, who is the image of God, should shine unto them."
- Proverbs 17:11, "An evil man seeketh only rebellion: therefore a cruel messenger shall be sent against him."

DANIELS PRAYER SEEKING GODS MERCY OVER THE NATIONS REBELLION

Daniel 9:4 And I prayed to the Lord my God, and made confession, and said, "O Lord, great and awesome God, who keeps His covenant and mercy with those who love Him, and with those who keep His commandments,

Daniel 9:5 we have sinned and committed iniquity, we have done wickedly and rebelled, even by departing from Your precepts and Your judgments.

Daniel 9:6 Neither have we heeded Your servants the prophets, who spoke in Your name to our kings and our princes, to our fathers and all the people of the land.

Daniel 9:7 O Lord, righteousness belongs to You, but to us shame of face, as it is this day—to the men of Judah, to the inhabitants of Jerusalem and all Israel, those near and those far off in all the countries to which You have driven them, because of the unfaithfulness which they have committed against You.

Daniel 9:8 "O Lord, to us belongs shame of face, to our kings, our princes, and our fathers, because we have sinned against You.

Daniel 9:9 To the Lord our God belong mercy and forgiveness, though we have rebelled against Him.

Daniel 9:10 We have not obeyed the voice of the Lord our God, to walk in His laws, which He set before us by His servants the prophets.

Daniel 9:11 Yes, all Israel has transgressed Your law, and has departed so as not to obey Your voice; therefore the curse and the oath written in the Law of Moses the servant of God have been poured out on us, because we have sinned against Him.

Daniel 9:12 And He has confirmed His words, which He spoke against us and against our judges who judged us, by bringing upon us a great disaster; for under the whole heaven such has never been done as what has been done to Jerusalem.

Daniel 9:13 "As it is written in the Law of Moses, all this disaster has come upon us; yet we have not made our prayer before the Lord our God, that we might turn from our iniquities and understand Your truth.

Daniel 9:14 Therefore the Lord has kept the disaster in mind, and brought it upon us; for the Lord our God is righteous in all the works which He does, though we have not obeyed His voice.

Daniel 9:15 And now, O Lord our God, who brought Your people out of the land of Egypt with a mighty hand, and made Yourself a name, as it is this day—we have sinned, we have done wickedly!

Daniel 9:16 "O Lord, according to all Your righteousness, I pray, let Your anger and Your fury be turned away from Your city Jerusalem, Your holy mountain; because for our sins, and for the iniquities of our fathers, Jerusalem and Your people are a reproach to all those around us.

Daniel 9:17 Now therefore, our God, hear the prayer of Your servant, and his supplications, and for the Lord's sake cause Your face to shine on Your sanctuary, which is desolate.

Daniel 9:18 O my God, incline Your ear and hear; open Your eyes and see our desolations, and the city which is called by Your name; for we do not present our supplications before You because of our righteous deeds, but because of Your great mercies.

Daniel 9:19 O Lord, hear! O Lord, forgive! O Lord, listen and act! Do not delay for Your own sake, my God, for Your city and Your people are called by Your name."

Also by Bliss

DEVOTIONAL
Consistent Bible Reading Plan
My Bible Study Journal
The Spirit Of Rebellion

Watch for more at www.theeblissempire.com.

About the Author

Sylvia Sande a.k.a Bliss is a lover of God and serves the LORD in the Childrens ministry at Harvest Family Church International in Kenya .Sylvia is an upcoming Christian author who seeks to write christian content mainly to inspire her generation and that to come.She is very passionate in the things of God and how to be better and grow passionately .

To connect with Sylvia ,reach her out on slysande17@gmail.com or sylviasande93@gmail.com

WhatsApp or Call +254795825427

Read more at www.theeblissempire.com.

www.ingramcontent.com/pod-product-compliance
Lightning Source LLC
Chambersburg PA
CBHW051906130726
47987CB00002B/997